PRAIS

RUNNING WIT.. ...- .....N

If you see me running, you better run too. The only time I run is when something really scary is chasing me. Angela Hunt is no different. But the things chasing her were not your grisly horror story monsters. A genetic predisposition to heart problems, a desire to be there for her daughters, and a realization that when it comes to bodies, more isn't better were the dogs snapping at her heels. She started the journey with a faithful hound, a good training book, a memory of an earlier time when she ran effortlessly, and, most importantly, a goal. The goal was beautiful in its simplicity—finish a marathon[...]

Each time Angela confronts a new obstacle and vaults over it, we the readers cheer a little louder. This is a story by an adult about adult things, but it is one you need to share with your sons and daughters. [...] Running with the Moon has gifts for all of us within its pages.
- *Chris Cochems*

I'm not interested in running, but I found things that inspired me in other endeavors. "But it doesn't matter" has to be one of the most useful mantras I've ever run across.[...] I finished the tale with tears in my eyes and vicarious victory in my heart. I can already think of people who need to read this[...]
- *Kimberly Wall*

RUNNING WITH THE MOON

RUNNING WITH THE

MOON

a Woman, a Dog, and 24 Weeks of Nights
to the
Los Angeles Marathon

☽ ○ ☾

ANGELA N. HUNT

HUNT PRESS • LOS ANGELES

Published by Hunt Press, Los Angeles, California.

www.huntpress.com

Printed in the United States of America

ISBN 978-0-9858954-5-7

10 9 8 7 6 5 4 3 2 1

FIRST EDITION

Dedication

For Jane, Grace, Winter, and Aurora

and

For any girl, anywhere, who has looked up and said,

"Watch me go."

Table of Contents

Stretch

When I first began Tweeting and posting on my blog and
Facebook about my marathon training, it got a lot of responses
and comments. But none more important at the outset than the
one that came to me through email. My friend, Jason, sent me
this email:

> *I have a request.*
>
> *Write a book about your training and running a marathon.
> Even a short book. Throw in ruminations about your mother
> insulting you about it, and about missing your father. Tell us
> about your girls, and publishing, and what it is to be a working
> mom with daughters in a world where women are still treated as
> second class citizens. Tie together running and writing and sci-fi
> and life in the way only you can.*
>
> *Title it "Run Like A Girl: blah blah blah" with the blah
> blahs being whatever you feel is right. Or whatever title works
> best.*
>
> *I would read the Hell out of that. I would hand a copy to
> Winter when she's old enough and tell her she can do anything.*

And I read that. And I smiled. And then the title of what I
really wanted to write hit me in the face and I realized that this
was the Universe slapping me with the big pink Salmon of
Wisdom again, asking me to do it. Because it's not just Winter
that I need to tell about my nights of training, a dog at my side,
the moon in my sky.

It is my own daughters. It's anyone's daughter who needs to hear: don't listen to the naysayers. Don't believe that you are constrained by the limits others try to lay on you. Put on your running shoes. Stretch out your bones. Find a companion.

And run.

Week 1 – Training Before Training

Moon phase: Waxing
Distance: as far as you can go in thirty minutes

Get out of the damn house

Go ahead.

Ask it. I know you're dying to. I can see it right there in your eyes.

Why a marathon?

Feel better?

Okay.

First answer: Why the hell not?

Second answer: A couple of things had happened in my life in 2011. It was coming up on my birthday and looking back, many competing thoughts pounded through my head. I had accomplished a hell of a lot of goals that had been with me for a very long time. I had written and published a trilogy of books. I had shown my photography all over the world. I was once more in pre-production on a movie, this time my first feature.

All the things that I had said as a teenager that I was going to do? The things that were going to be my big life work/I'll fucking show you/things?

Yeah.

Done.

Now what?

And a little voice said, *I'll tell you what. How about you stop talking about how you want to run the Iron Man some day and fucking get to it?*

And I had to admit. The little voice had a point.

It is one thing to say functionally your whole life, "Gee, wouldn't it be neat to run the Iron Man in Hawaii?" while watching the coverage from the safety of your couch. It is another to look down at your overly soft middle and go, "Hmm..."

It is also another thing to be painfully aware that a fatal heart attack killed your father and put your grandfather in the hospital, not once, but four times. It is another thing to have just buried that same grandfather that February. It is another thing to be 40, going on 41, and realize that if you don't take really good care of yourself, you might not be there for your daughters.

At least, these are all the things that ran through *my* head.

Because see, this wasn't a completely hare-brained idea I was having here.

Once upon a time, I ran. Yes, it was a million years ago, but I did. I ran five, ten, fifteen, sometimes even twenty miles every other day in my teens and 20s and I *loved* it. Running was freedom. Running was strength. Running was one of the only times in my life where no one was telling me what a failure I was or how lazy I was or how inadequate I was.

As long as I was running... Well. Let's just say that it was as close as I knew how to feel free in those days. So I did what I always do when faced with a new thing.

I went and bought a book.

A book, you say? Yes. A book. Specifically The Non-runner's Marathon Trainer by David Whitsett, Forrest Dolgener, and Tanjala Kole. It is exactly what it says on the tin. A training guide for those of us who do not already log 30 or 50 or 100 miles a week in road running. A guide for those of us who wake up one day and go, "Damn it, I better get to it." So when I talk about my mileage and training and all of that, this is where I'm coming from. If you're looking for a training guide, I cannot recommend it enough. It's aces.

But moving on.

So I had my manual. My map, if you will. I read the first few chapters. I went out and bought new running shoes, a sum that was more than I had spent on shoes that weren't designer in a dog's age.

And then I faced the first of many challenges.

Getting out of the fucking house.

It's one thing to decide that you are going to do something about your physical health. It is a very very different thing to have the shoes in hand. The work out clothes ready. And the first truth of marathon training slaps you in the face.

It is all in your head.

No. Really. It is. There are people who are blind who run marathons. Who are over 100-years-old. Who have braces on their legs. Who do it in wheelchairs. Who have literally been carried by others. I could tell you stories for days that would have you weeping at the indomitable spirit of humanity. All of this being predicated on the desire to run a marathon, anyone can run a marathon in some shape or form. Anyone can finish.

Note that I am not saying *win*.

I am saying *finish*.

Because in marathons ***that is the Win.*** Not being first. Not being the fastest. Not being the strongest. Just finishing. Y'know. Like life. And the first thing they tell you to do in training is to set this one goal. Not to run in x amount of time. To just finish. And to do that, you must make your first choice and set your first intention and convince your brain to get your body in motion.

You must get out of the fucking house and take your first steps.

It wasn't easy. The sensation of physical resistance that first night was intense. I was tired. I didn't feel good. I had a bazillion things to do. I missed my girls and I hadn't even left the house yet.

But then I looked at my soft middle again and I looked at my girls and I thought of my father. I thought about how I couldn't seem to walk anywhere anymore without it wearing me out. I remembered how I used to be able to go for days and loved the feel of the strength of my own body.

I wanted that shit back.

I took the dog's leash down from the wall hook and I called Maria. I went out the door. And that first night, I only walked.

Hey Jude

I kept going out. The schedule the book recommended was three nights every week, longer on Sundays, for four days total, Sunday being the only day I actually saw the sun to do it. Adding more running every time, learning to minimize the amount of time I walked. Maria was not fond of the more running. She is a lazy dog. She likes to amble. But she was game every time I picked up the pace, even if she did and does have an annoying habit of stopping suddenly to check things out and nearly jerking me off my feet. Though she does that less now. Apparently, my forward momentum is harder than it was at the beginning.

And then one night, I ran in the rain.

It happens. If you're committed, you run no matter the weather, no matter how shitty you feel, no matter how little "time" you supposedly have. This was one of those nights when it began to rain before I finished my time outside.

I turned for home. The rain fell like the lightest of touches. And *Hey Jude* from *Across the Universe* came up on the iPhone.

I still can't tell you why. I don't think it's important.

But in that moment, in that still night, the rain falling on my face, Joe Anderson singing in my ears, I began to weep.

I cried and I ran.

But I didn't stop.

When I got home, I felt lighter than I had felt in months.

Sometimes that's all you need. The rain to wash you clean. The voice to sing what's in your heart, even if it's not your own. The night to hide you. The feel of your body carrying you forward. A black dog at your heel, a constant kind shadow.

The rest is just stuff.

Week 2 - Come Run with Me

Moon Phase: Full
Distance: as far and as fast as you can go for thirty minutes

I have this horrible habit. I read ahead in books. Every book.
I'm not the kind of person who can just start and read straight
through. I read the last pages of books when I browse to see if
everyone dies. Because I know me. There are some kinds of
books that just make me miserably unhappy. Reading the end
doesn't spoil them for me, though my sister thinks I'm crazy for
skipping into the middle of things and the ends of books. I just
have to know if I'll be able to climb through the whole book and
get to the end with my faith in humanity still intact.

So, as you can imagine, I skipped ahead in the training guide.
I'm glad I did. Because earlier than later, I ran across the advice
they give for what to do when things on a run start to crater,
specifically: pain.

They offered the following phrase:

"Hello, [x], I've been expecting you. Come run with me."

They said to say it like you would to an old friend, open yourself
up to whatever it is, be it cold or heat or hills or pain... And
keep running. And it would make things easier.

Skeptic that I am, I went, "Huh. We'll see." But I filed the advice away in my head and went out and had the opportunity to try the phrase out. The most interesting thing happened. I can't begin to tell you how many nights I would find myself whispering to myself, "Hello, pain. I've been expecting you. Come run with me." And every time?

The pain would fade.

It didn't go away. But somehow, for some reason, embracing the discomfort, treating it as a friend and not as an enemy... I don't know. It made the pain a companion and not a saboteur. A difficult friend, not unlike the dog, but one that was making me stronger.

I began and have continued to use this one phrase in ways that are remarkable for how they reframe things that otherwise might have been just overwhelming or horrible or difficult. It was yet another example of how much of not just the training, but life itself was and is entirely in our heads. It makes you treat the world as a companion, not as an enemy.

It was, for me, a dramatic, profound, amazing, wonderful shift.

Hello, Life. I've been expecting you. Come run with me.

Week 3 - But It Doesn't Matter

Moon phase: Waning
Distance: as far and as fast as you can get in thirty minutes

Before I knew it, I could run for thirty minutes straight without wanting to die.

Three weeks fly by when you are running four nights of those weeks, every week. I looked up and realized that I had nailed down what the training guide said was the minimum for beginning the actual program. It advised two things. One: pick a marathon from the back of the guide (it had a list) that was four/five months out and sign up for it right away. Two: it was another piece of mental advice I snagged from reading ahead. And it went like this. Every time you had a negative thought (EVERY TIME), it said, add the words (either out loud or in your head) *"...but it doesn't matter."*

The weather is crap tonight...*but it doesn't matter.*

I feel like shit...*but it doesn't matter.*

I'm tired...*but it doesn't matter.*

And dear sweet gods and little fishes, what an enormous difference those four words made and continue to make for me.

Because, yes. Some nights, the weather was absolute crap. Too cold. Too wet. Too late. But it didn't matter. Some nights I felt absolutely wretched after a long day. But it didn't matter. Some nights my girls were fractious and brawling. But it didn't matter. Some nights I just wanted to sit on the couch, too damn tired for words. BUT IT DIDN'T MATTER.

Did I want to run the marathon or not? Was I quitting or was I just beginning? Because if I wanted to run? If I was just beginning?

It didn't matter what the weather was like. It didn't matter that I didn't feel good. It didn't matter that I was tired.

And y'know what?

All the negative stuff that we run all the time? All the excuses? All the platitudes we fill our heads with?

They don't matter either.

Those four words made me face things square on. How often I let negative emotions and negative thoughts keep me from things I really wanted. Experiences and activities and just, hell, life in general. When the reality was, all that negativity mattered less than nothing. There was no one with a gun to my head saying I couldn't do what I really wanted to do. Weather is weather. Run fast enough, you warm up. Even in ice cold rain. Get moving, even slow, and even if you feel bad, by the time you get to the end, you'll feel great because the endorphins will be flowing through you like the best drug high ever. Get moving, even tired, and you'll hit the end of the run feeling like you've had the best cup of coffee ever but without the jitters.

Don't get me wrong. I had days where I was so damn tired that by the end of the run, endorphins and all, I still felt like five miles of bad road. And I also felt like the Queen of the Entire Damn Universe. Because I had logged my time and my miles. The feeling of accomplishment filled me in ways that I didn't know it could and that I never had felt in my earlier years of running.

What's funny as all hell is that my friends began to comment on how suddenly much calmer I seemed. How things that used to wind me the hell up, suddenly seemed to roll off of me like water. It wasn't that I didn't get upset anymore. But it was a rational, reasonable type of response to things. Irritations and challenges weren't sending me into depressions or rages anymore. They were just happening and I was just dealing with stuff.

Because it didn't matter.

You know what *does* matter?

My girls.

My husband.

My sister.

My friends.

My family.

My art.

My life.

The rest? Yeah. It's all just stuff.

For this one bit of training advice alone, the guide was worth its weight in gold. I wish I had found it sooner. It is no understatement to say that this bit of guidance has changed my life.

I don't know if it has changed anyone else's life. Your mileage may vary. But my suspicion is, you may find it just as equally world changing if you give it a try.

Go ahead. Give it a whirl.

Week 4 - Where the Streets Have No Name

Moon phase: New
Distance: 3 – 4 – 3 – 5

And here's another funny bit to this story. It was during one of the night runs, thinking hard about this particular bit of advice that the iTunes shuffle chose to throw U2's *Where the Streets Have No Name* on the ear buds. I've always loved this song, for multiple reasons. As my husband would be the first to tell you, it's typically the first song the band plays as the beginning of the first of the encores during the live shows. And inevitably, as the Edge begins to play, Bono will start doing laps around the stage, *even though he has already been on stage, singing his heart out* **for two hours.**

He runs. That's some outrageous stamina.

And I realized I knew how he did it. It didn't matter if he was tired. When it was time to be On, Bono knew he had to be On, and his way to re-energize for the second half of the show?

Run.

And that was when that particular song became my marathon song.

Because if Bono could do that every night of every tour at his age, well, hell. I could finish a damn marathon.

Week 5 – 2.75 Miles to the End of Washington Pier

Moon phase: Waxing
Distance: 3 – 4 – 3 – 6

My week's runs settled into a pattern. I ran Tuesday, Thursday, Friday and Sunday, with Sunday reserved for the "long" runs, Saturday and Monday as dedicated rest/recovery days. These are critical. Long runs take it out of you. The body needs time to rest after things like that.

It was also the beginning of where my weeks would start to be consumed by mileage and the time to knock down such mileage. No longer thirty minutes and done. Now I had to go the distance, no matter the time. And that Thursday night's run was my first four-miler.

At the end of the run, I looked down at my GPS tracker and almost didn't believe my eyes. 12:58 min/mile pace.

Realize that up till then, I'd been averaging 13:40 and 13:50 on my pace. Slow. Healthy adults walk briskly at an average pace of 13 minutes per mile. I couldn't even run that fast. And here I shaved almost another whole minute off my pace and over a longer distance.

My friend, Charles, told me the next day, that even at his healthiest and when he was in the Infantry that was his pace for a run.

I didn't know who I was anymore or where I was finding the strength or the endurance. It just showed up, along with me and the dog, even on the nights where Maria and I would start out quick because we were both so damn cold our teeth chattered. Seriously. A dog's teeth can chatter. It's comedy gold.

As it says above, it is exactly 2.75 miles from my house to the end of the Washington Boulevard Pier. And if you time it right, it feels like you are running straight into the heart of the sunset. And if you are lucky, you will hit a point on the pier where suddenly you are surrounded by seabirds, lifting in flight, but at eye level, all flying in the same direction with you and you will feel like you are flying with them.

That Sunday, on my first long run, this is what happened to me.

Did I get high on that feeling?

How could I not?

The rest of the world falls away in moments like that. I ran home with a smile on my face. It didn't even feel like six miles.

Week 6 – Forerunner

Moon Phase: Full
Distance: 3 – 4 – 3 – 6

It has been less than 50 years since women have been included in marathons.

And it took Kathrine Switzer crashing the Boston in '67 to make that happen.

She only made it because other men running ran around her in a shell so the race organizers couldn't physically grab her and drag her out of the race. Jock Semple, the race organizer, specifically went chasing after her.

> *"Get the hell out of my race and give me those numbers."*

He is recorded as shouting this at her. Photographers caught the moment, her running on with the serene face of a Valkyrie, her clothes being pulled, even as other runners *turn to run back to help her*.

She didn't get the hell out of that race. Her boyfriend and other male runners kept pace with her for the entire marathon.

Kathrine would eventually go on to win the NYC Marathon with a time of 3:07:29.

You want to hear something even wilder? Since women have begun running the marathon and ultramarathon races, as a gender, they have made greater progress in less time than men. The longer the distance, the more even the odds become. Any race over thirty miles? It's an even split as to who will win. Men do not have the advantage.

Weaker sex, my ass.

The first time I read this story, I cried. Because I could imagine being Kathrine. I could imagine being driven by the desire to enter and run. I could imagine being afraid, because I know she must have been.

And I can imagine running anyway.

Women like Kathrine are owed an enormous debt. By everyone. For their defiance. For their courage. For the fact that nearly fifty years later, I didn't even think twice about entering my first marathon. That I didn't think twice about anyone telling me I couldn't do it because it wasn't allowed because of my fucking gender. They told me all sorts of other reasons for why I wouldn't make it, but that one fallacy wasn't thrown in my face.

And by the way?

To the men who ran with Kathrine that day? Whoever and wherever you are?

You are my heroes.

Thank you. For myself and my daughters, *thank you.*

Week 7 – Parenting is a Full Contact Sport

Moon Phase: Waning
Distance: 3 – 4 – 3 – 6

So there I am, working on getting ready to start nothing but running, no walking at all (I'd been walking the occasional block) with the next week of training when I go to turn in one night and another use for my running is made abundantly clear. This is a story concerning my youngest daughter, what I normally refer to as my Cute Bean Stories, the same way that I have Cute Mouse Stories to tell about her older sister.

I do not have a Cute Bean Story to tell you.

I have a Terrifying Bean Story to tell you. Which will only prove that Hyatt genetics are un-killable and my father is laughing himself sick on the astral.

One night, after my walk/run, just as I was turning in for bed, Grace used a brass bangle to A) destroy her nightlight; B) destroy the power outlet; C) (thankfully) trip the breaker.

She arc welded the bangle to the night light. It's sunk a good quarter inch into the prongs now and is one solid metal piece.

ARC WELDED.

Here. Let me show you a picture, which will do no justice to it.

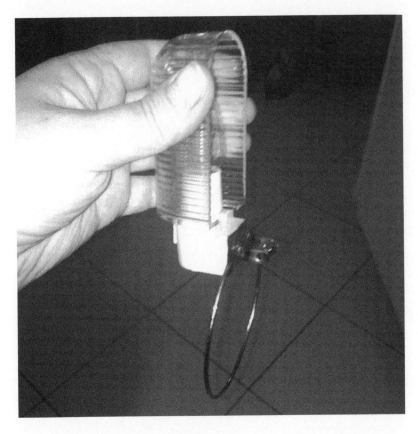

I was barely able to go to sleep after that.

I suggest you send your bribes in now. The world clearly has no chance. Her rule will be both adorable and terrifying. There is now duct tape over the outlet. The tape is covering the scorch marks around the defunct outlet on the wall. It took me forever to go to sleep and I made my husband promise on a stack of Bibles to not come to bed until he was *certain* that she was passed out.

I lay in bed after that, thinking, I can't call my grandparents or my father and ask, "How do I keep her from killing herself?!" When I ventured the question on the astral, all I heard was my father's laughter. Though I got the sense that he was *inordinately* proud of his granddaughter.

headdesk

He would be. Lightning was his stock in trade.

Arc. Welded.

Aiya.

This? This is up there with the hobby rocket my father launched as a teenager that nearly decapitated Grandpa and the nitrogen tri-iodide that he spilled and then forgot about till it dried on the laundry room floor to my Grandmother's great dismay. Grace is, without a single doubt, genetically and spiritually descended from her mad scientist grandfather.

goes to drink tequila out of flask when no one's looking

What does this have to do with running, you ask?

I took my worries and my troubles with me when I went out for the next run. All my fears. And even the black humor of the situation. While I remembered viscerally the feel of strength and well-being from running, I had forgotten something. It takes away, just as it gives.

It takes away stress. It takes away worry. In my case, it literally pounds tense muscles into submission and relaxation, insisting that the mind and body release its fears, because in the act of running, there is no room for anything else. There is only the moment. The night. The dog. Breathing. Heart beating. The shock of feet hitting the pavement.

It strips you clean.

And in regards as to parenting small children hell bent on destruction, it then gifts you with the patience to deal.

My daughters continue to exhibit the genetic gift of their inheritance. Inquisitive, sharp, curious minds. Here's another reason to run. It is not enough to just be a creature of intellect. The body requires stimulus, just like the mind. One of the Greek philosophers said that it was required to spend equal time in both gymnasia and academia. To put too much in one or the other was a deficit, leaving you either a muscle-bound moron or weakling of an academic. He exhorted people to choose balance. So to balance those sharp minds, I hope my running teaches my girls to exercise their bodies as much as their minds.

I don't think I have to really worry. After all, Jane has been dancing since she was three, Grace is about to take classes and has only two speeds: running and sleeping.

But like with all things in parenting (or so it seems), being the example is more important than telling the example.

Week 8 - Jens

Moon Phase: New
Distance: 3 – 4 – 3 – 6

And then Halloween kicked me in the teeth.

The night before, right before I went to bed, I found out that Jens H. Altmann had killed himself apparently a few days before that. He was a comic book creator, a novelist, a translator and commentator. He was my friend. Death doesn't change that.

I was one of his beta readers. We never got to physically meet, but we "met" on Warren Ellis' Engine forum back in the day and he was one of the core group of people who insisted I go to Italy when the opportunity came up in 2007.

But he had depression. That was obvious to me and it was sometimes hard talking to him, because he lived in the hole. I told him to keep swinging, to not give up, even when he told me it was pointless and that he felt he should just admit he was a total failure and give up on it all. He said he wasn't going to write anything new. I asked him not to give up. I told him that I believed in him.

And then he rather vanished on the internet. He did that from time to time. I hoped he was just regrouping and getting himself together.

Apparently, it was too much to hope for.

I sent him an email the morning of Halloween. I had to. I won't share that here.

I'm still angry.

Not at Jens.

Oh, for so many other reasons. I've never had patience for people who cause grief, or suffering; who ostracize others; who pretend to be too cool for school; who denigrate others' enthusiasms; the glossy cruelty. This isn't the first of my friends I've lost to suicide, to the black maw at the bottom of the pit, the despairing thing. Watched them crumple under the callousness that the world can dish out sometimes. I'm fucking sick and tired of losing friends this way. I'm fucking sick and tired of howling into the wind about this.

But I'll keep screaming defiance at Bitch Entropy.

I don't have to like any of this. This world is duality, the bitter with the sweet, and Entropy always wins. But oh, I'm going to make Her motherfucking work for it. I grieved and alternated between going numb and having it wear off.

Samhain ended up being very interesting that night. I didn't expect to have someone else to throw in the cauldron.

I didn't expect to spend that week running not just with the dog, but with the ghosts of all my Dead. It was the only way I was able to come to any peace with what had happened.

I still miss you, Jens.

Week 9 - NaNoWriMo

Moon Phase: Waxing
Distance: 3 – 4 – 3 – 6

And then it was time for the glorious mayhem that is National Novel Writing Month. I've been doing it since 2004 and it is my devotional of choice when it comes to my writing. Out of all the years I've done, only twice have I not finished and the first was my first year and the second was that I was just pregnant with the Mouse and throwing up all the time.

Good times.

I thank NaNoWriMo for being the thing that took me from being one of the world's slowest writers (we're talking Thomas Harris slow) and turning me into someone who could write to a frikken' deadline. I was so upset by not finishing my first year, that when 2005 rolled around, I buckled down and just pounded.

It was a revelation.

It's not for everyone. But for those of us with competitive spirits and a desire for community, a desire to know we're not alone in our solitary madnesses, it is the best thing that has ever happened to me or my writing. Some years are hard. Broken Rainbow I had to fight for every word, tooth and nail. Alice Assassin was fun, but I never did more than just what I had to write every day.

2011, I couldn't seem to stop writing, even with the marathon training, the words were coming so fast. It was like NaNoWriMo helped me find that door in the page that Stephen King talks about, helped me pick the lock, open it up and finally, finally, finally helped me fall through the page.

It was a gift.

And it felt strange. Because here I was. Training for the marathon *and* pounding words onto the page for NaNoWriMo *and* getting ready for Thanksgiving *and* getting ready for my first genre convention in years which was also going to be the first official convention that my tiny little genre press was going to attend in an official capacity.

I should have imploded from the stress.

I didn't.

The training guide, amusingly enough, talked about this phenomenon. Again and again, they had students that during the training found that they were more organized, more competent with their time, and more accomplished when they were training than at any other time in their lives. That the physical act of carving out the necessary time to run pared away all the non-essential things in their lives and left only the things that mattered.

So let me be the first to tell you, if no one has, and you are a fellow NaNo-er and you're thinking about training for a marathon, but wondering if it's too much on top of everything November throws at a person. I have only one thing to say to you:

Go for it.

Week 10 – So What's My Story?

Moon Phase: Full
Distance: 3 – 4 – 3 – 6

And then I got sick. And boy, did that fucking suck.

The Bad Brain reared its ugly head for the first time in weeks. I laid it at the feet of the head cold that I couldn't seem to shake, as the training for the marathon left me feeling pretty balanced. But it's hard to stay in positive headspace when full of snot.

If you read the advice out there about how to be a working artist, there's this thing where they say talk about who you are.

Simple advice. Except what if you don't know who you are anymore?

I'm a lot of things. Mother. Wife. Artist. Author. Madam Publisher. Filmmaker. Photographer. Painter. Manager. Office drudge. None of them by themselves is all of me. Even taken all together, they're still not all of me. They're part of me.

They're not who I am.

Call it a midlife crisis if that'll make you feel better. I did turn forty the year before. It was that and it was more and it was less than that.

Like I said, I had done a lot of the things I said I wanted to do when I was younger. I had published multiple books and short stories. I had had big gallery shows. I had shown in Europe. I had made multiple movies. I had gotten to take some rather spectacular photos. I had painted. I had sold work. I had learned how to do yoga and fence very poorly. I had met some of my childhood idols. I had walked fire. More than once. I had given birth to two daughters.

I hadn't run a triathlon yet though.

But.

I am not the things that I do.

Which is all a long way of saying, I had done all these things and I found that I was now standing around going, "Now what?"

Seriously.

Now what?

I was cranking away on wordcount for NaNo, which was gratifying and helped offset the despair.

But what was really cool was my friend, Vicky Jo, saying to me when I told her about my state of Now What? She said something to the effect of it being fertile ground for something new to appear. And to ask myself: "Wouldn't it be nice if...?"

It was a great help. It gave me some tiny directions to go in. Like getting sushi for lunch and pounding more words on the novel that seemed hell-bent on unsettling the crap out of me.

And, oh yeah. More running.

Week 11 - Running at the Speed of Dolphin

Moon Phase: Waning
Distance: 3 – 4 – 3 – 7

That Sunday's run was then another minor revelation. Seven miles and it was just no big deal. Took time, yeah, but… Physically? No big deal. I began to really really believe with every fiber of my being that not only would I run the marathon come March, but I'd just motor. Not fast. I don't need to be fast. But I can see running the last mile to the finish line, my face hurting from smiling.

It was a really great visualization.

It certainly gave me the strength to dig out from the overwhelm and sorrow of the previous weeks. Things still loomed.

But I ran. And off in the waves, going in the same direction as me, at the same speed, dolphins arched through the waves so close that I swear I could have waded out and started swimming with them. And the Earth abided with me as I ran. And the sun shone. And my girls hugged me when I got home.

Week 12 – Shut Down

Moon Phase: New
Distance: 3 – 5 – 3 – 8

Strangely or maybe not, mid-November wasn't just a case of existential angst for just me.

The entire nation was (and continues to be) in its grip. In a small park in New York City, a group of people had declared themselves Occupy Wall Street. They also called themselves the 99%, invoking the percentage of US citizens who don't make over a million dollars a year. Who struggle to make ends meet. Who struggle to keep their homes. Who, to paraphrase the movie *Network,* were mad as hell and not going to take it anymore; the rampant social injustice they saw at work not only in their country, but in the world. And from their small flame, a hundred other fires were sparked.

Including one that would call itself Occupy Los Angeles.

My dayjob was two blocks from the Occupation. Every day of their residence, I heard or saw evidence of them. And then, nationwide, the Occupation called for a mass action. That mass action took place on November 17th, 2011.

It took me an hour and a half to get to the dayjob that day. The Occupiers shut down downtown Los Angeles. HARD.

When I crossed the pedestrian bridge from the garage to my building, this is what I saw:

Eerie.

Like something out of The Omega Man. I kept expecting Charlton Heston to come screaming up in his Mustang. Normally that intersection is bumper to bumper parking lot commuter traffic.

In the distance, I could hear chanting, yelling and sirens.

Never again say to me that we can't make a difference.

It may be slow. It may take years. It may be as endurance-provoking as any marathon. But to me, like the idea of Now What? being the fertile ground of opportunity, the empty streets of LA sent a frisson of hope through my body.

Things were, *are*, changing.

We just have to keep putting one foot in front of the other.

Week 13 – Holiday Time

Moon Phase: Waxing
Distance: 3 – 5 – 3 – 10

And then the holidays were in full swing.

Got home one night and was incapable of writing, which had
happened the night before as well, but I did run, which was all that
mattered. Did not hit the scheduled 3 miles, but came damn close.
Poor dog I think was certain I was torturing her. But it was temperate
and warm and pleasant and with the fingernail moon in the sky, it was
not too hard to believe myself running with Artemis and her hounds.

Run kicked my ass, and after getting the girls scrubbed and myself
scrubbed, that was all she wrote. I was literally too tired to even eat
any of my pumpkin pie.

I know. What's wrong with me?

Week 14 – Car Troubles

Moon Phase: Full
Distance: 4 – 5 – 4 – 11

And then, two days before the anniversary of my father's death, my car, a 2001 Ford Mustang (it's a convertible and I named her Andromeda Ascendant, full disclosure) would not start. Turned out that the fuel pump was completely gone, which is very normal in a Ford of that age (also normal for most GMs). To replace the pump and filter (because you don't want to burn out a new pump), pay for labor and the tow that got the car to the garage, it came out to $1000 and some change once tax was factored in of money I did not have.

Yeah.

Momma needed some help.

I also knew most people were bidding on things for Magick4Terri at the time, a benefit for Terri Windling. If you do not know who she is, let me give a brief thumbnail that will not come even *remotely* close to describing what a grace she is to the science fiction and fantasy community. Terri is writer and editor, but also muse to a whole generation of writers, especially *women* writers. Her book, The Wood Wife, was one of the novels that when I read it, I sat and cried and wondered when she'd snuck into my life and read all my logbooks.

As a result, most focus was on helping her in her time of need, which was far more important than my car troubles, but I asked for help. I put up a print sale. I told everyone I could think of that I needed help.

And got it.

I tell this story, because too often we get into trouble and we think no one will help us, that we are beneath or beyond saving. I had believed that for years until 2007 when too many people dragged me out of that and sent me to Florence to show my art to the world.

I learned my lesson. Since that time, when in trouble or doubt, I speak up. And *every time, help arrives.*

Not sometimes. Not maybe. EVERY TIME.

Sometimes it looks weird. Sometimes it's sideways. Sometimes it's help for something else that doesn't look like it should help me at all, but it shows up anyway and suddenly...well. It was really the help I needed.

And at this iteration, not only did the help show up, but so did this message:

Keep running.

At this point, my loved ones and supporters, knew I was training. They were more concerned than I was that I would lose focus and stop running. There was no chance of that, because the running was already starting to give me myself back, but the gratitude that I felt at being shoved out the virtual door...

Honestly, there are no words.

Help and help and help, over and over.

The Mustang still needs work.[1] But it runs. Just like I do. And it wouldn't have happened if I had kept my mouth shut.

---

[1] *Sadly, the Mustang is no more. Early in 2012, she blew her engine and that was all she wrote. I miss her like burning, but for a short while, she was mine.*

Week 15 - More Winter Sorrows

Moon Phase: Waning
Distance: 4 – 6 – 4 – 12

And then even more sad news arrived. My dear friend Mindy's grandfather died. Will Townsend, a dear friend of my husband's, died in the wee hours of one morning, struck and killed by a drunk driver.

Other news came in about my family that left me gutted.

But I can share this, and I share it even now.

Tell your loved ones how much they mean to you. Life is just too damn short.

As for me, I did what I was doing then. I stayed with my husband the night he heard about Will because he needed me. I ran later in the evening and it was a hard run, one where you just put your head down and gut that fucker out. I came home and made post-modern sugar cookies (lumpy forms with sprinkles; hey, it's art, man). I may have possibly eaten a huge chunk of bread.

But most of all, I held people in the light. I lit a candle against the dark. I kissed my girls.

And I kept running, pounding my sorrows into the pavement.

The hits kept coming. I couldn't ever seem to find the ground, because the hit that followed in the form of family news was a wakeup call, more than anything else. Not for me, because I felt pretty damn awake, but even so, it was pretty loud.

The reasons for all of the anvils falling from orbit were obscure to me at the time, but one overriding one was not.

As my dear friend, James, would say: we are the product of our cumulative choices.

I would add: we are not alone. I kept hearing and seeing bits of the movie, *Contact*, in my head.

> *You're an interesting species. An interesting mix. You're capable of such beautiful dreams, and such horrible nightmares. You feel so lost, so cut off, so alone, only you're not. See, in all our searching, the only thing we've found that makes the emptiness bearable, is each other.*

And that's why I could stay standing and moving forward. Because I knew and I continue to know we have each other.

It is enough.

Week 16 - More Car Troubles

Moon Phase: New
Distance: 4 – 6 – 4 – 14

So, the year turned and 2011 realized it hadn't shit on me enough. The van that the Ant drives the girls around in broke down and began leaking LOTS of fluid all over the driveway.

Yeah.

That was no bueno.

I couldn't get it to the mechanic till the next week, as that was when I got paid, and even so, well, I hadn't offset all of the fuel pump repair. So I extended the print sale I had started running for the fuel pump for another month and remember how I said help shows up?

It showed up again.

But oh. If I hadn't had running.

At this point, December was so awful in so many ways, that I wanted to pretend that the holidays hadn't even happened. If it hadn't been for the fact that the girls' sheer unalloyed joy over Christmas was unaffected by what was going on in my life, well... I don't know. I don't really want to think about it.

I clung to the fact that Christmas kept its magick for my girls. I pounded pavement. I prayed to the unending moon over me. I poured my troubles into the dog's ears, because even if Maria wasn't the best running partner, with her constant need to stop and jerk me off my feet, well, she *was* the world's best listener.

A dog never judges. A dog never tells you what to do. A dog, especially as sweet and neurotic and patient as Maria, will look up at you with big brown eyes and if you are weeping, she will lick your cheek as if to say, "Everything will be all right."

Week 17 – The Downside of Flow

Moon Phase: Waxing
Distance: 5 – 8 – 5 – 16

And then one Sunday, I inadvertently ran 18.14 miles, instead of the 16 miles that I was supposed to log.

How, you may ask, do you overshoot your turnaround by a whole mile?

You run in flow. And forget to pop out occasionally to check your mileage.

Oops.

So what is flow? Actually, you already know what it is. It's that place of unconscious competence where your mind goes away and your body does what it does. Any commuter will tell you about it. You make the drive home so many times, your mind just goes away and before you know it, you're home but don't remember driving any of it. *That's* flow. It's moving meditation.

I'm really good at flow. I've been doing some form of it since I was fourteen. Marathon training deliberately invokes flow, because when you're in it, not only do you run better, but you actually run *faster*. I know. It makes no sense. But when your mind isn't screaming the whole way about "Oh my fucking gods, how many miles?" your body gets down to the brass tacks of just doing it.

But being really good at flow and at a point in my training where nothing hurts and I'm apparently really really strong means, I popped out of flow, looked at my mileage and went, "Oh fuck."

Because instead of increasing two miles from last week's run to this one, I'd increased by four. That's non-trivial.

The last two miles home were hard. HARD.

But I did it.

And more importantly?

Eighteen miles is the magic number. If you can run eighteen miles, you can run a marathon. As of that day, my body told me it was ready. I could run the marathon. Now it was just about building more strength, more endurance, and remembering to not go so far into flow that I missed my turnarounds.

This was and is the body I remember having. I was so damn happy to have it back. Especially since, once upon a time, there were people who said I would never walk without pain after my car accident, let alone run.

This was and is me.

Running.

Week 18 – Moon, Regret, Accomplishment

Moon Phase: Full
Distance: 5 – 8 – 5 – 16

And we turned for home one night, Maria and I, coming back out on the long straightaway, the last mile of one of the five-miler, and what should I see before us, rising from the horizon, glorious and huge and round and orange?

The full moon sailing into the clear indigo night sky.

Ia! Ia! Artemis!

The Moon saw us home and lifted my heart right out of my chest, the cure to a very long, hard year.

So the year turned and looking back, 2011 fucking sucked. Up there with 2008 for years that just were murder. Again, just happy as hell to see the ass end of it.

I mean, yeah, it wasn't all awful. I got to meet Kyle Cassidy in the flesh for the first time and he did me the honor of taking some of the best photos of me that I have ever seen. That alone is worth an enormous pile of gratitude.

But I felt like I spent most of 2011 regretting things. I don't want that to happen ever again, if I can at all help it. It's not a way to live.

Aside from finishing the Alice Assassin series, the occasional snapshot and being invited to be the wedding photographer for dear friends, I did no new photography in 2011 and that above all else…hurt. Not that finishing Alice was anything to sneeze at. But I couldn't justify the expense of another heavy production shoot. As most of you know, I am a set heavy/prop heavy/theatrical photographer. It's how I itch my filmmaking scratchiness without resorting to total film insanity. And I did not get to indulge in it to my full delight.

And painting, well. I finished the covers for Dark Lightning and Broken Rainbow. I was smashed in the head with the idea for a new one. I'm not going to push for more than that, because like the photography, my time just dwindled in 2011.

The press, however, continued to make huge bloody strides. In a year of awful, it was the shining, gleaming thing of wonder and I am so grateful for it. Along with beginning to run at the end of the year, the press kept *me* going, not the other way around. We published two calendars and six books. Which was HUGE. 2012, we planned to publish twelve books hopefully, and hopefully another calendar. That was nothing to sneeze at.

I did write a screenplay for the first time in years and I wrote another novel. It felt routine. So right there, time to push the envelope. I don't ever want this to feel like routine. I've fought too hard for this life of the writer. It's too precious to treat like routine. The same way I never want the running to feel like something I do with zero mindfulness. It's all too important, this life we are given.

So in spite of too many deaths and too much sorrow and health scares and drama, much was accomplished.

Looking back over the year was necessary. Because by the end of December, I was feeling too ground down by the bad. Making myself look back, I was able to see the good. The way that the training insisted that I add, "But it doesn't matter," to every negative thing I thought or said. I was finally able to look at all that had happened and for the first time ever when I said, "but it doesn't matter…"

I meant it.

My locus-of-control was once more back inside my body, not out in the world.

Yes, metric tons of bad things had happened. But I couldn't control those things. I could only control myself. My reactions. My emotions. My actions. And in the midst of some of the stronger challenges of my life, running gave me my rock and I clung to that sucker.

I ran out of 2011.

And once I did that last look over my shoulder to see what I was leaving behind, I didn't look back again.

Week 19 – More Lion than Gazelle

Moon Phase: Waning
Distance: 5 – 8 – 5 – 16

> *Every morning in Africa, a gazelle wakes up.*
> *It knows it must outrun the fastest lion or it will be killed.*
> *Every morning in Africa, a lion wakes up.*
> *It knows that it must run faster than the slowest gazelle, or it will starve.*
> *It doesn't matter whether you're a lion or a gazelle*
> *when the sun comes up you'd better be running.*
> *(But, unless you're a runner, you won't understand.)*
> *-Anon*

Yes.

You'd better be running.

This is why I run, right here. I'm not the fastest runner in the world. I get paced all the gods-be-damned time when I'm out on my long runs. My short runs were (and continue to be) at night and no one else is on the road for the most part. At those times, I run with the Moon, and the dog, and She never outpaces me, and Maria just perseveres till I look down at her and say, "Last mile, Maria."

The Moon just keeps me under Her eye. The dog stays constant at my heel.

But the long runs are different. I get paced. But this particular week's long run, an interesting thing happened. It was long enough finally, that I started seeing the same runners both heading out and coming back.

And they were walking.

They couldn't keep the pace they had set.

I was still running, my slow, steady, ground-eating lope. And for the first time ever, I paced *them*.

So, here is today's lesson: it's not about how fast you go. Can you keep the pace you are setting? Because it's not just Aesop and his fable telling you this, it's a real world fact. Find your own pace. Keep to it. Run your own race. If you do, you'll leave the gazelles far far behind.

listens to the Lion roaring in her heart

It was a very good thing I found the piece of inspiration when I did, because right after that, the husband got laid off from work. It ended up being the best thing (again) that could have happened to him, and I was not overly concerned, but coming on the heels of vehicles breaking and the remaining vehicle needing service and family health issues and hitting my own mental wall with the marathon training…

You can't make yourself be positive. All you can do is control how you react to things. I am not one for tail spins.

And I was reminded of something. Anger is also energy, just like fear. I am fine with my anger. It doesn't frighten me. I also watch Kobe Bryant put up 40 point games, largely because someone has pissed him off.

It was just my turn to put up a 40 point game.

That seemed to be the thing I needed to kick down my mental wall. After that, the training improved. My runs didn't get much faster, but my attitude got better. The husband was on the hustle and was getting good responses to his resume, so that was one less stressor. The family health chimera continued to loom, but it was getting dealt with.

I kept on keeping on.

Then I acquired an epic set of blisters on my right foot pinkie toe and thought about missing a run that week to give it time to heal a little more. I didn't. I read up on treating blisters for runners, followed the instructions (trust me, you don't want to know if you are squeamish, and if you are a runner, you know already), and got my ass out the door anyway.

One of the night runs hurt like a motherfucker. I don't know if I didn't stretch enough or what, but holy crunchy frog, it sucked, not that my pace showed it, so go me. Quads were killing me and the blisters on my right pinky toe continued to be painful little bitches. I did more work on my foot and seemed to catch the last blister (seriously, I had blisters under my blisters).

The next day my foot just felt raw, not *"Oh hai, I am under your epidermis and here to fucking torture you!"*

So. Progress.

Pro-tip for other returning or newbie runners: micropore tape is your friend. Sand off your callouses and tape your feet before you run. You will thank me.

The next day, I was sore and tired and meant to do as little as possible after work. Another rest day, because my brain might have re-grown and the Post Novel Ennui might have lessened, but the body required nothing more than to not move and to drink and eat all the things. The day after that was a five-mile run.

So. It had been a busy, busy, busy week. Lost Tuesday to torrential freezing rain, one of the few times I did not go out to run in it, so I did that week's training runs back to back to back, which I worried about, but which the body responded to with not even a hiccup. It was *wonderful.* But it did mean that on the 8-miler nights at this point, I got nothing else done but running. Which was actually fine. It was and is more than enough to get home, love my family and then run 8 miles under the full moon.

At this point, not much else was going on. I ran. I continued to write. My camera and easel languished. But the marathon was less than six weeks away. I knew I would need them then, for after.

The sixteen-miler that week-end was an interesting one in that physically, I was pretty fine, barring the blisters. Yes, as I got to the last three miles, I was feeling *tired*. But that wasn't what was eating me.

It was all the bullshit in my head.

It's amazing the crap judgments we run on ourselves. That day, it was all about how I wasn't running fast enough, never mind the blisters, never mind that I ached like an old lady, it didn't matter. Every time someone passed me, the Critic in the head would start up on how we should speed up, we were going too slow, yadda yadda yadda…

Except…

In comparison to what?

The part of me that knew better came back very quickly and thankfully with, "According to whom?"

So here was this run's lesson.

This isn't a speed race. It's an endurance race. The point is to *finish*. And this is true about so many damn things. Who the fuck cares if you get there first? Because I have news for you. Someone's already been there first. ALWAYS. But not everyone finishes.

Slow doesn't matter.

DONE matters.

And right then? As of that day, I had run more than half a marathon. The Critic could suck it.

So Sunday's run was fucking brutal, mentally. After the fact, I could only think that I did not get enough sleep on Saturday, both nap and night-wise. All other components of my training were right where they needed to be. It was just my sleep was not there and I found that I chafed against the restriction, because every minute I was and am not awake is a minute I was and am not making something new.

I resented it and I still resent it.

But I needed to be able to run effectively.

It was a trade off. I just had to fucking do it.

Week 20 - Fat

Moon Phase: Full
Distance: 5 8 5 18

Valentine's Day week and what normally would have been my Tuesday night run got pushed to Wednesday, because yes, family comes before training. It meant that I ran another week back to back to back, but whatever. The previous week I proved that I could do it. That week, I would just do it again.

And oh, what a joy. The first five-miler? The night had gotten bitter again. Gone was the unseasonable warm. Winter found its fangs again and took a bite and Maria and I scampered that first mile, doing all we could to get warm.

But best of all?

This was the night where I felt like a well-oiled machine. Like I could run forever. Like I was made of nothing but strength and energy.

Orion and Jupiter shown cold and clear over our heads.

Glorious.

This is why I started running again. This is why I committed to training for the marathon. I remembered this feeling. I remembered feeling like this all the damn time and how good it felt and there was nothing better.

When I got home, I tried on the jeans that had been sitting on the top shelf of my closet for the last four years.

And they fit.

Here are the ramifications of this. My whole life, all I ever heard from my mother was that the reason she was fat was because she had had me. Until she got pregnant, she had been thin and beautiful and then she had a baby and that made her fat. Not obese. Not overweight. No. That was never the word she used. She insisted on one thing:

I made her fat.

Imagine saying that to your child, to any child. But I heard this my entire childhood.

Standing there in my pre-pregnancy jeans, with a commitment in my head and heart to not just run the marathon but to keep running forever?

Yeah. I don't know how many times I have to prove to myself that my mother and all the people like her are liars. Probably as many times as it takes. But here it is again. If you were told something like this? If you've been told that having children will destroy your body and you will never get it back? That you should just give up and not even try?

Don't be fooled. They are all motherfucking liars. You can get it back, if you really want it. Just find something you love to do that gets you moving. And go do that.

Sanderlings and Seal

Sunday rolled around and the 18-miler went pretty well, though the tide was in at the beach, so it was tough going. No hard pack sand to run on, on the way out, and I hurt like hell the next day. Sore and very tired.

But.

On the way out, rolling around on the beach, an adolescent seal was chilling when I went by. I have never been that close to one. Literally three feet. And it just looked at me and chattered like a cat and then waddled back into the ocean, when I looked back over my shoulder, all brown and sleek and glossy-eyed. Between that visitation and the tiny tiny white seabirds that look like animated sea foam, running alongside me as I pounded up the beach...

Yeah.

It was hard and I was tired, but my soul was full.

Love is Paper

I deal and process through paperwork.

When times are hard, I write and I file and I fill out paperwork. And 2011, like I said, had some giant things to process and only in February was I finally released and in a place where I could talk about the family health terror I had been carrying for four months.

I preface all of what I write next with this: Barrie, my sister, is fine. And there's a reason I have to lead with this. A little after Thanksgiving, she found a large lump in her breast.

Barrie does not have health insurance. My dayjob would not let me add her as a dependent.

This is part of the reason why the end of 2011 was such hell for all of us. Scrambling to get her to the Venice Family Clinic, one of the few free clinics in California. Getting her to the imaging center. And then waiting. And waiting. And waiting. For what was eventually a clean bill of health.

[Through it all, I must especially give thanks and shower blessings on Joyce, our friend from the Santa Monica dogpark. I don't know what we would have done without her support.]

The entire incident terrified me. We lost my Aunt Jan to breast cancer. I have too many friends who are survivors or children of survivors. But most of all, I couldn't bear to think of what would happen to Barrie's body of work, should the diagnosis have come back as the worst. An accomplished illustrator and writer, she has an enormous literary estate and just that year I had watched several artists die, their estates in shambles, their survivors left to the wind.

But then I remembered Neil Gaiman posting his will form for writers. And I channeled my fear into paper and defiance against the final dark that we face in our lives. Because what Neil had posted? It wasn't enough. It was merely a start. And I knew too many people who would do only that and think they were done.

You are not.

Barrie's scare crystallized it all for me. It wasn't just about her. It was about every single one of my creative friends who doesn't have insurance. Who wouldn't even know where to start.

But I do, because I sit in the beige cube at the dayjob and I touched these papers every day. The way that the rich plan for the inevitable future. How, touching ten thin sheets of paper, handed to me from one of the attorneys I admired the most, I saw written in black and white the depth of love and continuing protection from beyond death. Because the words weren't always about money. Buried in these documents, were often sudden transcendent, brief paragraphs of prose that had nothing to do with the law, or estates, or property.

They were the last breath and wishes of someone who wanted to make sure that whoever was left behind, wasn't abandoned.

And I remember, still with anger, how my father did none of these things and left my Margie Mom in penury.

I just...

I just couldn't let that happen, not if it was in my power to prevent it. Not for anyone I love. Not for any of you that I can reach with my words.

So here are the things that you need to do and you need to do now, especially if you are an artist of any stripe. They are specific to California, but if you search on Google, you will find forms for your state. You will need to prepare the following:

> *Simple Will*
>
> *Creative Property Trust (this goes with the Simple Will)*
>
> *Advance Medical Directive*
>
> *Durable Power of Attorney*

You need *all* of these forms. A will is not enough. You must have a trust spelled out, either a testamentary trust or a living trust. You must have an advance medical directive. You must have a durable power of attorney. Filing fees will cost a nominal amount. It is a small fucking price to pay to take care of whoever is left behind. If you give a shit *at all* about the ones you love and your legacy, you will do these things now.

Because you may not be here tomorrow.

My father was gone at 59.

Will, my husband's friend, was gone at 33.

I dodged a bullet on a diagnosis that could have been an aggressive and fatal brain tumor.

Barrie dodged a bullet on a diagnosis that could have been the same disease that took my Aunt Jan.

Don't fuck around. Get this shit done. Now.

Because love is paper and your hand held over your loved ones in protection even unto your death.

I took this energy with me into the weekend and knocked down the 18-miler on Sunday. Only one more lay ahead of me on the next Sunday and then time to begin the taper, the period of time where I would allow my muscles to heal in prep for the marathon in (holy shit) 25 days.

Week 21 – 24

Moon Phase: Waning
Distance: 5 8 5 18

24 days till Race Day.

I was terrified.

Not of finishing. Not of quitting. Not of pain or the distance or the time it would take.

I was afraid of the unknown.

I had dreamed about running a marathon since I was fourteen-years-old. In 24 days, it would no longer be a dream. I would have done it. By hook or by crook, strong or hobbling, I would cross that finish line.

And I didn't really know what would happen after that.

Everything would change and nothing would change. Running this marathon wouldn't save the world. But I do know one thing. Running this marathon was saving *me*.

About this time, my dear friend, Robin, asked where people could gather to cheer me on, come Race Day. His question left me joyously speechless. I had asked Matthew and the girls and Barrie and Heidi to meet me at the finish line. I had planned to upload my bib number into the online app that would allow folks to send videos and messages to two video boards on the race route that were triggered by the GPS chip in my racing bib.

But then more and more of my friends piled on the thread, wanting to know the same thing. (Robin had asked on Facebook.)

This is why they tell you to tell everyone that you are going to run the marathon.

There are more people than you can possibly imagine pulling for you, cheering you on, wishing you every joy and success. For every jerk telling you it can't be done, there are at least ten who believe in you.

Find those people. Keep them close. Cherish them.

When you do?

They'll be the ones waiting for you at the finish line, cheering you on.

And for the record, I'm cheering you on too.

Then came a night that week where the run was murder. I discovered the hard way that the strawberry Clif gel blocks were a migraine trigger and spent the first three miles of the 8-miler working on not throwing up. At which point, the Imitrex finally kicked in, but yeah. I don't recommend doing that. And *noto bene:* for those of you with citrus migraine triggers, avoid the strawberry Clif gel blocks. The cran-razz are safe though.

I had a bit of the migraine hangover the morning after and my head still hurt a bit, but I managed.

And the run was all I accomplished that night. Which was plenty. This was the last high mileage weeks before the marathon. After Sunday, tapering had to begin.

Almost there...

Week 22 - 20

Moon Phase: New Moon
Distance: 5 8 5 9

20 days till Race Day.

The last 18-miler lay behind me. The weekly runs remained the same for that week, but next Sunday was only nine miles. I know. "Only." But seriously, nine miles after eighteen isn't nothing, but it's not the same. It's just nine miles. 108 minutes, give or take.

And to think. Three months ago, I was wondering how the hell I was going to get my ass back up to running five miles.

And then the training was all in my head.

My right knee ached, my body said that it was tired, and my stomach wanted a caprese salad. My body was lying to me. If I listened to my body, I would not go out. I would stay home.

I did not stay home.

We are so much more than flesh and bone. If I learned anything over those last twenty-one weeks, it was that. I had now gone out so many times when my body made whiny little noises at me, only to have Mile 3 vanish under my feet and suddenly feel like Queen Hippolyta. Tireless. Strong. Relaxed.

I am more than just a body.

Thank the almighty gods.

And then there were the nights where everything went pancake-shaped.

Everything happened one Thursday, including the thermal coil failing on the water heater for the house and by the time I finished triage for everything going on...

It was almost 9 PM.

This is where the battle for miles and the battle for adequate sleep got waged. I ended up only running 3.5 miles and still ended up in bed just shy of midnight which sucked. It didn't help that after Tuesday's run, Maria was limping. Not in a really bad way, but in that, I strained something way. I was worried she would not be up for running on Thursday, though there was no sign of it, and she ran fine with me when we did go out.

Because, let's face it. I'm not an idiot. I'm not running alone, at night. Not without bear-grade pepper spray or the dog.

Upshot of all of this is, the evening was beyond stressful. I went out the door with my head full of worry and fear and anger and not even half a mile into the run?

Gone.

As I tweeted when I got home that night: A body in motion can not worry.

Week 23 - 12

Moon Phase: Waxing
Distance: 3 5 3 8

Twelve days till the marathon.

Twelve days. Twelve days is really no time at all.

Like the publication of my trilogy and the birth of my girls, this was one more milestone my father would miss. His death wasn't the sharp horrible stabbing thing that it once was, but the bitter and the sweet, those remained.

If I am at all athletic, it is because of him. My mother was not at all. But Pop, he played football in high school. In his 30s, he was the one who buckled down during the divorce, started eating right, got a gym membership, and for a while, took me along with him when he would go to the gym after work, the two of us doing the stationary bikes and the weight stations. He didn't think I was crazy when I ran in high school. He didn't think twice that I biked to and from school a distance that other parents drove their kids.

His expectation and my expectation of myself was that I could do it.

So I did it.

I know he is proud of me. I know he would both think I was a little crazy for wanting to run marathons at this age and that he would also think that it was exactly the sort of thing I should do. For a man who loved food and idleness, he also understood the need for a sound body. Unfortunately, the food and idleness and the genetic predisposition to heart disease won over the intellectual understanding.

And this is always in the back of my head.

It was in the back of my head when I went out the door all those weeks before. His genetic predisposition is *my* genetic predisposition. My grandfather had four heart attacks and four quadruple bypasses. My father had *one* fatal heart attack. There is other history, not mine to share.

It all boils down to one thing.

As hard as this was, and it was *hard* some days, it is exponentially easier than the alternative.

This wasn't about training my legs. It was about saving my heart. It was about keeping it beating for as long as I can, come hook or crook.

So I continue to eat my oatmeal in the morning rather than the eggs and bacon I want. In this week, I ran the first three miles of the week, the overall mileage in the taper dropping to nineteen miles.

And I cherished the beat when I heard my heart make itself loud enough to be heard in my ears. Because I've already dodged a couple of bullets aimed at my health. No need to put me in front of Disease's gun again, when I know it's already gunning for me.

Week 24 – The Last Week

Moon Phase: Waning
Distance: 3 3 walk 3

The last week before Race Day passed in the cliché blur. I don't recall much of it. I remember alternating bouts of nerves and excitement. I remember starting to chat up Helga, the only one of my dayjob co-workers also running the marathon, though she was in a different department. She was a huge inspiration, as she had twenty years on me and this was her nineteenth marathon. She had run her first at the age of 50. She made me look like a piker.

We shared encouragement and smiles that my other co-workers did not understand. It was pretty clear they thought us both crazy as drunken loons.

I was fine with that. I wasn't doing it for their approval.

And as Race Day got closer and closer, I found myself growing calmer and calmer. Whatever would happen, would happen. No matter what did happen, I knew I was going to leave it all on the course. That's all I could do.

Then Friday rolled around and it was time to go down to the race expo and pick up my bib and gear bag.

Race Expo

Driving out to Dodger Stadium that Friday was a solitary and quiet thing for me. I decided to go alone, having taken the day off from work. The drive was quiet and uneventful and getting to the stadium wasn't too bad, traffic wise, a blessing in Los Angeles.

The quiet went out the window when I got to the expo.

The first thing that hits you is the noise. Music blaring over the PA. Announcements. A TON of bodies, people there for the booths and other runners there looking for their gear bag. I wandered a little before heading to the tent where they were handing bibs out. I have to say this for the LA Honda Marathon. They were organized as all get out. Took me not even five minutes to get my bib, my gear bag and my participant shirt.

And then...

I didn't know what to do with myself.

I took a picture of my bib.

And I honestly felt a little lost at that point.

All that was left was the waiting. But I'm not good at waiting. So I took my iPhone and went and took more pictures.

In two days, that would be my spot.

I couldn't stop smiling.

Race Day

Moon Phase: Waxing - new beginnings, the time to invoke, the phase sacred to Artemis
Distance: 26.2

I don't know how to write about the marathon.

But that's probably the best place to start. I don't know how to do this. I will do it anyway.

My alarm went off at 2:45 AM, Sunday morning, March 18th, 2012, and I rolled out of bed like I had been jabbed with an electric cattle prod. I had been worried that I would have trouble waking up. I shouldn't have. I was immediately AWAKE.

Still in the bed, Matthew slept and I quietly picked up my clothes and gear that I had laid out next to me on the nightstand, things and clothes I had laid out the week before. I brushed my teeth. I washed my face. I slathered on the friction balm at the points that I knew would chafe. I pulled on my race clothes. I had already taped up my feet the night before, along with painting my toenails a brilliant scarlet. I couldn't wear makeup and run, so my toes would wear my war paint. I slipped on the metatarsal support pads I'd gotten. Slipped on my socks and picked up my shoes.

After that, I just tried to breathe and stretch until it was time to get in the car. The house was heavy with silence, everyone sleeping, even the dog.

But the cats were not.

Each one of them came to touch my nose with theirs as I lay on the floor and stretched. It was like they knew I was up to Something. They normally have no time for me. Not so this time. Lady Bast's avatars blessed me and watched me prepare.

Checked my gear one last time. Put on my shoes. Took a photo for Instagram. Filled my water bottle with Black Blood of the Earth and milk to drink as it got closer to Race Time. Bundled up against the cold.

And without a backward glance, gear bag in hand, I stepped out of the house.

Los Angeles at 3:45 in the morning is a ghost town.

Desolate. Lonely. Quiet in a way that is hard to describe. Again, Omega Man level of empty. I made it from the house to Santa Monica in under nine minutes and just a quarter mile out from my destination, joined a small river of cars, heading the same direction. Without question, other marathoners.

In the absolute pre-dawn dark, we drove our cars into the lot. Parked. Climbed out.

I joined another river, this one of silent walkers, one here, two there, all of us heading for the shuttles that would take us to Dodger Stadium. No one spoke. And it was at this moment that I felt for the first time and the most strongly that we were joined. Devotees of an ancient sport, disciples of Athena, though who knew if anyone else felt that way but me. In the dark and the cold, we walked.

Ten minutes later, we reached the veritable fleet of shuttle buses waiting for us.

Here, the nerves set in. Small conversations. Nervous laughter. I climbed on the bus and a woman my age sat next to me, Martine. We talked about our children. We talked about the weather. She was a consistent half-marathon runner and this was her first full.

"I'm hoping to do it in four and a half hours," Martine said.

I laughed.

"I'll be happy if I come in under six!"

And that's when the bus passed the ramp for Dodger Stadium off the 110. It was closed to all traffic.

"This is bullshit!" our bus driver exclaimed in a heavy Spanish accent and I have to admit, I laughed like a hyena. Here it was, a little after four in the morning and we were officially off course, lost and nowhere near the stadium. Granted, it only lasted a few minutes. The driver got us to the 5 and then to the other approach to the stadium, but for a brief time, we were all very very happy to be on a bus that early and not one of the later ones, where we might have been late for the start time.

Now the bus joined a river of other buses heading into the stadium parking lot.

And suddenly and again, it was not quiet anymore.

The minute we parked, music and live DJs echoed through the bowl that surrounds Dodger Stadium. Runners everywhere. I climbed off and just as I hit the asphalt, Martine turned to me.

"Have a great run!" she said and disappeared into the crowd.

And just like that. I was alone.

I had a moment of not quite knowing what to do with myself. It was ridiculously too early to go and take a spot in the open seed corral. I wasn't hungry, though there was a place where they were handing out bagels and bananas and water, according to what had been in my race day info.

I saw many people streaming into the stadium proper and I figured I'd do the same as I didn't have any other idea.

The stadium was lit up like it was for a Dodger game. And on the big Jumbotron screen, they ran video of celebrities and previous marathoners talking about their favorite mile of the marathon in between sponsor shout outs. Sitting there in the stands with hundreds of other runners, waiting for it to be closer to time to start, who should be one of those clips, but Kobe Bryant.

I have to admit, I grinned like a loon, listening to Kobe talk about Mile 26 being his favorite. How it's all about getting down to the wire and putting it all on the line. How much he loved those clutch moments and that energy. Considering how he had been one of my mental inspirations on the nights when getting out the door had been hard, when I hurt, when little dings made me slow, hearing him then settled my nerves.

It's funny, but for so many people, we were fairly quiet.

Not silent. Hushed conversations went on. But most of the people around me napped or clearly meditated. Took pictures of themselves or their friends in front of the vast green of the baseball field. Huddled under trash bags and blankets, because it was bitter cold, though the rain didn't appear to be making an appearance. I chatted up a lovely man who had literally decided just that weekend to run the marathon, being out there for a job interview, already an experienced marathoner and figured, what the hey, since he was in town, he'd run. Impressed the crap out of me.

Another guy who I ended up sitting next to, me in a seat, him on the ground, talked about the weather and nothing of consequence. But I felt connected to him, just like I felt connected to all the others waiting for it to be time to make our way to the corrals.

We huddled there in the dark, illuminated by the enormous klieg lights. And we waited.

And then it was time to get ready.

You have no sense of how many bodies make up 26,000 people, until you are standing in a marathon corral, waiting to run.

When I took my place in the Open Seed Corral at the 12:00 marker, I was one of a handful. But as the time grew closer, the next thing I knew, I was packed in with so many people that I could neither move forward, back or to the side.

Remember my claustrophobia?

Yeah. This was no fun for me. I pretty much had to do my breathing exercises and keep shifting from foot to foot, because even with all the bodies, it was still ridiculously cold, telling myself I was safe and not trapped.

As we waited, the other segments of the marathon began to take off. The wheelchair racers. The women elite runners. The men elite runners. Each sent off to the sound of a piercing airhorn.

And then us.

Here's the thing.

When 26,000 people start to move forward, you better be moving forward with them. The tide of bodies carried me forward, first at only a walking pace. And then, because we were so packed in, suddenly with no apparent outward signal, we were running.

You can't set your own pace at this point. You are packed in like lemmings. I had to run and luckily it wasn't too much off my own pace, but frankly, it was terrifying. I was sharply aware that any fall and there was no way to avoid getting trampled and taking others down with me. Adrenalin flooded into my system even more, and chilled cold muscles even further.

But two tenths into it, we hit our first downhill and the crowd thinned and the sun broke out from the clouds and...

I was running in my first marathon.

I wish so hard that I could viscerally share those miles with everyone. Words... Words slip out of my fingers, like elusive starlings, like slippery fish. We were one enormous, giant running animal. We were a river. We were an ocean, a rushing tide literally heading for the sea.

And every half mile there was some wondrous form of support.

Water stations and blessed porta-potties.

Young men and women with big sheets of cardboard smeared with Vaseline for those who needed aid for their friction burns.

The gorgeous, riotous lion dancers in Chinatown.

The taiko drummers at the top of Bunker Hill.

The gypsy belly dancers in Silver Lake.

The reggae band, hell, *all* of the bands out there playing their hearts out and yelling us on.

The drag queen cheerleaders in West Hollywood in their matching outfits.

The signs. Oh my gods, the signs. "Run like you stole something," "Free Beer at the Finish Line," and my personal favorite, "Worst Parade EVER," which made me nearly fall over laughing.

It was almost too much at times. The noise. The cheering. The yelling. It didn't stop, though it thinned out as the day went on. I think small armies actively waging war might be the only thing louder.

Certain miles stand out in my memory more than others.

Mile 5 we hit our first Time Clock and I realized I was way off my pace. Amusingly enough, we *all* surged forward. I was not alone in thinking, "Oh shit, gotta pick up the pace."

Then Mile 8 came around and the first of the ASICS video boards.

One of the incredibly awesome things about the marathon was that ASICS, one of the sponsors, had set up two video boards, one at Mile 8 and one at Mile 18, that were linked to a website, where supporters could upload video and photos and messages to encourage their runner if they couldn't physically be at the marathon.

I had forwarded the link to every single person I could think of that mattered to me and then quietly put it out of my mind, so I wouldn't hamster over it.

Ahead of me, runners crossed the telemetry pad in the road and one or two messages would pop up.

And then I hit it and I could barely keep up with the number of messages that flashed at me: Miss Lisa's margarita glass, Victoria's Scorpion King art, Shadow's video that had no sound for some reason, and two others that I can't even remember. Only Lisa's jumped out at me, one part specifically:

The only way out is through.

I laughed and laughed for almost a quarter of a mile after that, unable to catch my breath from joy.

That was the end of joy for a long while.

Around Mile 13, I started to feel it. The first tongue of fatigue, licking at my muscles and my lungs. I was going slower than I wanted to and it was taking me longer than I wanted and the individual miles seemed to be longer than any single mile I had run in training. I knew it was all in my head, but I started to despair that I hadn't trained hard enough. I hadn't run far enough.

Here was where the mental training took over.

I chanted my mantras. I remembered all of the positive things my family and friends had said to me. But above all, I chanted this:

I am fearless. I am unstoppable. I am relentless. I am stronger than this. I am a marathoner.

And I pushed on.

But closing on Mile 18, I started to hurt. My right knee started yelling pain and I had to add to the mantra, *hello, pain, come run with me.* I don't remember what the last Time Clock had said at that point, but it was very clear to me that I was going to come in over seven hours and my heart was just lead in my chest. I couldn't believe I was creeping so slow, but there it was.

And then I hit the video board at Mile 18.

Oh.

I can't even write about it without crying.

Again, the bombardment of messages, but this time, there were folks cheering *my name.* Watchers at the side of the road, pulling it off the board and yelling at me to "Keep going! You can do it, Anji!"

And then Shadow's video came back on and it had sound this time, and the last thing his message said:

"I know you've got this, babe."

I sobbed for the next quarter mile, running my heart out.

As if it wasn't enough that Mile 18 had reduced me to tears, Mile 19 conspired to do the same.

I left Beverly Hills behind and headed into Century City, alternating running and walking, the pain a constant howl at this point. With seven miles to go and the wind beginning to pick up, at this point I was seriously wondering what I had gotten myself into, but at the same time, I was still just pushing myself forward.

And that's when I saw them.

There, standing in the middle of Santa Monica Boulevard, a Marine veteran and his daughter, high-fiving every runner that went by, shouting exhortation to keep running. I can't write about them without tearing up. He still had that military haircut and wore an old USMC sweatshirt. His daughter wore gray sweats and smiled and shouted with him, but nowhere near as loud as this man. He had a voice that you could hear across a battlefield.

As I ran by at my turtle pace, we slapped hands and he looked me straight in the eye, his own the most amazing, piercing blue eyes I've ever seen, and shouted:

"Keep going! You're almost there! Remember! Finishing is winning!"

Finishing is winning.

Gods. I needed to hear that so badly at that point. Because oh yes, the Broken Brain had just started to go back into raging at how slow I was going. And just like that, his words shut it up. I was able to find my inner locus of control again. I was able to get back into silently chanting my cadence. I picked up the pace and kept going.

It didn't seem possible, but it actually got *harder* after that.

At one point around Mile 21 or 22, I thought, *oh gods, I don't know if I can make it.* Except it was immediately followed by this thought: *So are we quitting?*

NO.

Then shut up and keep going.

But even with that resolve, by the time I made San Vicente Boulevard and the last two/three miles, the wind had begun to blow directly at us out of the west at a constant 20 mph, with frequent 45 mph gusts.

Think about that for a minute.

At this point, I had been walking for at least three miles, unable to run faster than walking. I was exhausted. I was limping. And here was this howling, mad thing, blowing straight into our bodies, freezing cold. It was blowing so hard, it had blown all the inflatable mile markers down.

Except three.

Mile 24, Mile 25, and Mile 26.

Seeing those big blue arches over the course lifts your heart in ways nothing else can. And I saw the Time Marker for Mile 24 and couldn't believe it. Even with walking, I had somehow shaved 20 minutes off my split. Instead of coming in at over 7 and a half hours, I was going to make it to the Finish Line closer to 7.

My despair left me and a new determination replaced it.

And then I saw the arch for Mile 26.

I still don't know where I found it in me. But somehow, I began to run again. I remember thinking very clearly that I was going to be damned if I was going to finish my first marathon, walking.

At one point, the wind was such a physical force, that it literally felt like throwing my body into a brick wall and that I was making no headway. I tucked my chin down and pushed, furious at the wind, and made the turn from San Vicente onto Ocean Avenue.

And there it was, in the distance, point two miles away.

The Finish Line.

The wind tried to blow me off my feet, over and over. I actually accelerated. I ran and suddenly there were people cheering again. Shouting us all on.

And before I knew it, I was there, and I saw the two telemetry pads on the ground.

And I don't know how I did it, but I ran, jumped into the air, jumped on to the first pad and then jumped even *harder* on the second pad and...

I *roared.*

Above me, startled laughter jerked my head up. The race photographers were all staring at me. I couldn't help it, I grinned and shouted back:

"That was fucking HARD!"

And that made them laugh too.

Whatever had pushed me that last two tenths of a mile, left me at that point. I called my husband, trying to find him.

"We're at the family reunion area," he said when I got through, even as a race photographer asked me to lift my medal and take my photo. "You have to walk a few more blocks."

"Okay," I remember saying, even as I just wanted to fall down.

It was a gauntlet to get out of the race area. People handing me food, a survival blanket emblazoned with the marathon and Honda logos. (I still have it.) Stopping to get my gear bag from the pick up location. But then I finally reached the end of it all and stepped into the family reunion area, scanning and swaying on my feet.

Matthew came out of the crowd. He had spotted me first. He was wearing his Lakers championship sweatshirt, a concession to my obvious victory, slow or otherwise. I walked into his arms and burst into tears.

That night, I drank a bottle of champagne and sat in the bathtub, drinking it, and afterwards ate an enormous plate of enchiladas and chile rellenos. It didn't feel real.

It still doesn't feel real.

In the Shadow of Marathon

Moon Phase: ☽ ◯ ☾
Distance: ∞

Being back at the dayjob was beyond surreal.

I had taken the day after the marathon off and had spent the day mostly sleeping like the dead. But the next day I was back at work, moving like a cripple, and feeling completely disjointed with reality.

People treated me differently. They wanted to see my medal. They wanted to know my time. The number of times I heard, "Oh, I could never do that!" went without count and each time, all I could think was two things: if you think you can't, you can't, and of course you could do it, if you wanted it enough.

Anyone can do it.

But you have to want it. You have to want it more than anything.

And isn't that just a general rule for life?

I still don't know what I want to be when I grow up. I'm slowly rediscovering myself and setting new goals, because that's the only solution to reaching your goals in the first place. First, realizing that I had basically aimed way too damn low in the first place, and second, challenging myself to dream bigger and go into the world larger than I ever have before. It's scary as all hell. It's also how I have always dreamed of living my life.

But the same way that the last two miles of the marathon felt like they would never end, I know I will get where I want to go now, once I decide where I want to go. I just have to put my head down, lean into the wind, and keep putting one foot in front of the other.

So.

Let me leave you with one more story...

Pretend, if you will, that you stand at Marathon in Greece. It is August 490 BC. You have led your army to victory over the Persians and you are weary but victorious. Back home, in Athens, you know your peers wait for news, fearful of the battle's outcome. You turn to your best messenger, who has also fought in the battle, steadfast at your side.

Pheidippides.

You tell him to get the news to Athens. And oh, he does. He runs the entire distance without stopping, an achievement never before accomplished in recorded history at that time, and bursts into the assembly, exclaiming "Νενικήκαμεν!" before collapsing and dying.

We run for, and in memory, of him.

Νενικήκαμεν!

We have won.

Printed in Great Britain
by Amazon.co.uk, Ltd.,
Marston Gate.